The Teddy Bear Journal II

This journal begins on the fifth day of June 1988. I decided to write down some of the things that happen when we are together, Janelle so that someday you can read about it all by yourself. I selected this book because I thought you would enjoy the "teddies." You are five months old and are growing up so fast. This weekend we went to great grandma Willoughby's and as soon as we got back in town we went right over to see you. Your smile when you see us tells me that you're happy to see us. The feeling I have is one of complete joy. You are showing a lot of interest in my glasses that hang around my neck and try to grab them. Today you got new NIKE hightops from uncle Leroy and Aunt Sharon and of course you want to give them the taste test. We brought you a new outfit but it looks like it has to go back because you are growing so fast. I love you.

Grammy

HAPPY BIRTHDAY TEDDY

Thursday June 16, 1988

You came over tonight with your mom and dad for dinner. It's always so much fun to see you because you smile a lot. I try to do silly things to make you laugh. You love to watch the fan go around. Tonight you talked to Allison on the phone and tried to eat the phone. Finally as I carried you around you went to sleep. That's when it's so sweet to watch and kiss you. And when I took you out to the car you didn't even wake up. You are getting so noisy. We can tell you love to hear your own voice. I love you,

Grammy

Like angels, fairies, and elves, Teddies are creatures constructed of love and dreams—and are therefore pure and deserving of endless life.

—JANE SELLMAN

June 26, 1988 Sunday,

Grandpa and I spent the day (Saturday) watching Daddy play softball. We enjoy doing that a lot. It is just like all the times that we would spend hours watching and and traveling to baseball games. You had a cold and didn't sleep very well Friday night and even though you were a good girl Saturday the weather wasn't as good as it could have been. Your mother asked us if we would like to take you home with us. While we didn't shout "yes" inside we were pretty excited. We made your bed up on the love seat and propped the hide-a-bed cushions along the edge. Your mommy said you would probably wake up several times during the night so we were ready. At 2:45 AM I heard your little squeak and got up to put your "bink" in your mouth. You went smack, smack and fell asleep again. I woke up at 4:00AM and listened for you to wake up and decided to go and check on you. You were still on dream land. At 6:00 I heard a little squeak from you and brought you to bed. You snuggled down

The Teddy bear: Heart-grabbing mix of trust and doubt ineffable . . . Little soft
thing sent forth to make his simple way in a world so slow to hug.

—JEANNE WYLER TOROSIAN

and fell asleep again. Grandpa and
I watched you sleep.
Morning bath was fun. We decided
you were no longer a tadpole but a polliwog.
Grandpa gave you the bath and you
splashed and splashed. He said he couldn't
see because his glasses were all wet. We decided
to take you down town so that we could
maybe "bump into someone" while you were
with us. We went to the Flea Market to look for
treasures. A visit to Dick and Jenny's was fun too.
Dick let you throw straw coasters off the coffee
table. Your mommy & daddy came to pick you
up around 3:00 and we were lonesome after
you left.

Bears are great look-outs when you're raiding the refrigerator late at night.

—DAWN BEARE

Fourth of July weekend 1988. We spent the long weekend with your parents, cousins Rod, Karen, Bradey and Linsey and Aunt Allison at Sun River. Part of that time we were at Vaughn and Jacquitta's home at Metolius Meadows. It was the first time that a lot of people had seen you and everyone thought you were so pretty. Your big brown eyes and quick smile that wins strangers hearts worked on company and relatives alike. You have become pretty chatty with your babbling. There's a certain way you have of holding up your mouth and champing on your gums that makes everyone laugh, and the more we laugh the more you "talk." Linsay decided that she wanted to try your pacifier out. She managed to pull it out of your mouth and plopped it in her mouth. You tried to pull it back

it Linsay was the strongest
he finally got board.
ce when Linsay was crying
ou tried to cry of course we
hought that was pretty funny.
ne morning your mother brought you in
o wake us up. When we hear your little
squeal its easy to wake up happy. On the
ay home we stopped in Sisters, Oregon and
unt Allison shared blackberry yogurt with
ou. You love icecream and yogurt just like
your mommy. Your daddy thinks you are pretty
neat too. He carried you in the backpack and
the love for you is all over his face.

Now that I'm all grown up, I can buy any old Teddy bear I want—except the old Teddy bear I want.

—WILLIAM STERNMAN

Any Teddy bear who is at all important
should be hugged immediately.

—TED MENTEN

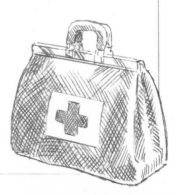

What is it about this inanimate object of fur and stuffing that makes it so hard to part with? As children, we were acutely aware of just how much our bears loved us, and we filled their ears with our daily doings and deepest confidences. How could one grow up and not take along this dearest of companions?

—SARAH McCLELLAN

Remember when I said Teddy can't sleep without me?
Well, truth is, I can't sleep without Teddy.

—WEBSTER PAPADAPOLIS

A row of Teddy bears sitting in a toyshop, all one size, all one price. Yet how different each is from the next. Some look gay, some look sad. Some look standoffish, some look lovable. And one in particular, that one over there, has a specially endearing expression. Yes, that is the one we would like, please.

—CHRISTOPHER MILNE

What is the secret of Teddy bears' instant success and enduring popularity? Very simply, they are irresistible—even those who've had their fur loved off or their paws injured.

—PEGGY BIALOSKY
and ALAN BIALOSKY

His name is Teddy—Teddy Bear—and he's as stable an institution as motherhood and apple pie, and probably as indestructible.

—MARVIN SCOTT

They're things that can give us comfort and peace—that can soothe us—in a world that doesn't always seem to offer much comfort and peace. They are, I think, the very essence of life itself.

—PAUL C. HORTON, M.D.

Baths really aren't much fun for bears, although
you will rarely hear them complain.

—MARLENE YOUNGREN

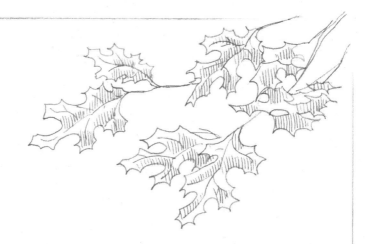

It is the charm of Teddy bears that they cannot be bored.

—TED MENTEN

Exercising did not come easily to Malcolm, for he was a stout bear and no longer young, and his furry stomach had a tiresome habit of getting in the way when he bent over. But a bear, even a stuffed one, had to keep himself in shape, especially after he had been dumped unceremoniously into a toy box in the attic.

—BARBARA DILLON

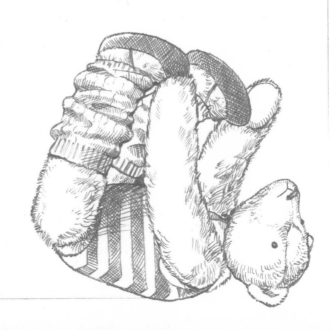

One day, when I was all grown up and sad, I happened to meet Teddy in the attic. Suddenly the years dropped away, and I felt young and loved again.

—HELEN FREISER

To a child, Teddy is a bridge between a human being and an animal. He doesn't mind being taken for a walk, dressed in ridiculous hats, or even being read to. You can blame him for anything, and he won't deny it. His marvellous face expresses anything a child wants to feel or hear.

—PETER BULL

Teddy bears are remarkably adaptable. How many other life forms can survive being kicked out of bed in the middle of the night, thrown in the washing machine with the dirty socks, and fed a constant diet of Crayolas and Play-Doh?

—SARAH McCLELLAN

No bear should be shelved too long.
It's terrible on the stuffing!

—SARAH McCLELLAN

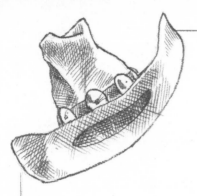

Our prescription for the good life is a chicken in every pot, a car in every garage, and a Teddy bear in every heart.

—GAIL RAZNOV

Sure, people like the way Teddies look. But it's the hugs they've inspired, the smiles they've invoked, and the love they've created that have made Teddy bears a worldwide symbol of caring.

—JAMES D. NELSON

You might say that growing up without a Teddy bear to hug would be like having a December without Christmas.

—MARVIN SCOTT

I didn't know if my husband would understand about my Teddy bear, who's been sharing my bed since I was four. But they had a long talk, and my husband discovered some things about Teddy that even I didn't know—like some nights Teddy would rather watch TV all night in the living room.

—LAURIE DILSON

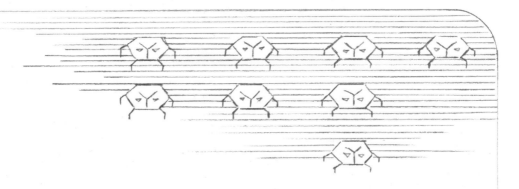

Teddy bears are more human than other stuffed animals. They seem very knowledgeable; they know what's going on.

—ANONYMOUS

Learn to listen like a Teddy bear,
  With ears open and mouth closed tight.
Learn to forgive like a Teddy bear,
  With heart open, not caring who is right.
Learn to love like a Teddy bear,
  With arms open and imperfect eyesight!

—SARAH McCLELLAN

Bearlonging (bār·lông·ĭng) n: An eager, strong, or earnest craving for Teddy bears.

—BEAR TRACKS MAGAZINE

My Smokey the Bear has been dragged along carpets, dressed up in doll clothes, and doctored with my plastic medical kit. He has sat on my bed in every house, apartment, and dorm I've lived in. When I had my tonsils out, he went to the hospital with me—all the way to the operating room. He has lost his belt, badge, shovel, and hat. His fur is a little thin in places, but his dignity is still intact.

—JANE SELLMAN

What poverty not to have had a Teddy bear!

Bears help people get through hard times. They have gone to the hospital and climbed mountains with their owners. During exams, women carry their bears in their pocketbooks; men keep them in their pockets.

—MARTHA HEWSON

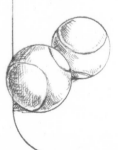

The bears are taking over our house, and we love it. They are really fascinating
creatures and seem to cast a magic spell over all they come in contact with.

—MARIE DICKERSON

(The Teddy bear) can be bumped and thumped and thrashed about without the least injurious effect. One might infer that rough-and-tumble qualities like these would fit the Teddy bear exclusively for the society of little boys. But such is not the case: he is clasped tightly to the heart of every little girl.

—CAROLINE TICKNOR

A Teddy bear's virtue is that he cannot love himself, only others.

—TED MENTEN

SPEED
LIMIT
25

YIELD

STOP

X·ING

Good bears are love made visible.

—MARTHA USREY

When a child loves you for a long, long time, not just to play with, but REALLY loves you, then you become Real. Generally, by the time you are Real, most of your hair has been loved off, and you get loose in the joints and very shabby. But these things don't matter at all, because once you are Real, you can't be ugly— except to people who don't understand.

—MARGERY WILLIAMS

There's just something about a Teddy bear that's impossible to explain. When you hold one in your arms, you get a feeling of love, comfort, and security. It's almost supernatural.

—JAMES OWNBY

Teddy sits in his own chair, staring at nothing, taking it all in.

—WILLIAM STERNMAN

. . . A quality Teddy bear, properly cared for, will last indefinitely. Some have already survived not only wars but a depression, smallpox, polio, diphtheria, and emotional trials and tribulations.

—PEGGY BIALOSKY
and ALAN BIALOSKY

My Teddy is never short on comfort and advice, yet he refuses to come forth with criticism.

—MARIANNE PONTICIAN

In our years of researching and collecting Teddy bears, we have encountered several bears who hold college degrees, having attended classes in their owners' pockets. At Dartmouth College, for example, a degree was given to one New Hampshirite—and her Teddy. Dressed in traditional cap and gown, he was in her arms as she got her diploma.

—PEGGY BIALOSKY
and ALAN BIALOSKY

When Mama took my Teddy away, she said it was time for me to grow up. Silly mother, not to know how wise a bear can be!

—WILLIAM STERNMAN

A Teddy bear is happiness and healing
in a child-sized furry package.

—CAROL-LYNN RÖSSEL WAUGH

How many children, do you suppose, have carried a lifelong resentment of parents responsible for the surreptitious removal of their Teddy bears?

—JOHN ZIFF

Even though there's a rip and tear in your Teddy bear, his love will not fall out.

—EVE FRANCES GIGLIOTTI
and ELAINE CLAIRE GIGLIOTTI

Good evening. Tonight, you will enter a world where promises are kept, dreams become real, and friends are forever: The Teddy Bear Zone.

—JAMES D. NELSON

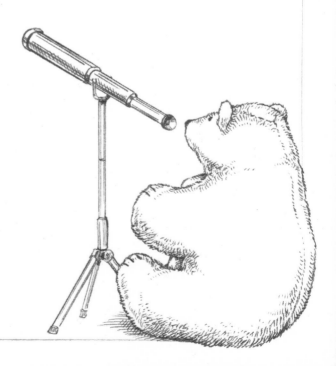

I like specific shapes and textures—and gestures—that describe a character in a toy. It's more exciting to be able to touch bear-like footpads or the complexities of a nose that is different from our own.

—CHARLENE KINSER

Does Tussah Bear have a philosophy on life? I think so. It's something like, "Love hard and love only one person; stay with them as long as they want you, and never leave them alone. Be prepared to venture out into the world with them, and never be afraid."

—JENNIFER PAULSON

Just knowing that your Teddy bear is home waiting at the day's end makes each day happier.

—TED MENTEN